HUNGARIAN TEXTILES

The object of this series is to present a Survey of World Textiles, each volume dealing with a separate country. The undermentioned are either published or in course of preparation.

Other volumes are to follow and will be announced from time to time.

HUNGARIAN TEXTILES

by

MAGDA GÁBOR

F. LEWIS, PUBLISHERS, LIMITED

LEIGH-ON-SEA

Introduction

HUNGARY TODAY joins the countries having a highly developed textile industry, her foreign trading companies regularly supplying textile fabrics and garments to eighty countries. These exported items are therefore considerable, even on a world scale. It was not always so; the Hungarian textile industry has had to travel a long way to reach its present high level. The manufacture of textiles was highly organized and developed in Britain and other West European countries when, in Hungary, it had but set out on its initial stages.

It was not until 1752 that the first Hungarian factory to produce cotton fabrics was established at Sasvár, and by 1805 fourteen thousand workers were engaged in its weaving mills.

The first important textile works of the Hungarian capital was the silk factory of the Valero Brothers, and in 1784 Ferenc Goldberger established his blue dyeing works at Óbuda, one of the suburbs of today's Budapest. The workshop, whose plant consisted of three vats and three hand-operated presses at that time, has grown into the present Goldberger Works, which can be described as perhaps the most famous textile works in Hungary, a factory which celebrated the 175th anniversary of its foundation in 1959.

To a certain extent the history of the Goldberger Works may be considered the history of the Hungarian textile industry, the way and the rate of its development being but a reflection of the whole textile trade in Hungary. As early as in the first decades after its foundation, the Goldberger Works attained great success with its products both in its home trade and in the foreign markets of the world.

In 1842, at the First National Industrial Exhibition, the exhibits from the Goldberger Works were awarded a gold medal. The diploma given with this distinction testifies to the fact that as early as a hundred years ago the factory produced textile goods which were exported from Hungary. Among other things, the following words are quoted from this diploma: 'The factory produces 120 kinds of articles, supplying them not only to the home market but to foreign markets as well'.

In addition to the Balkan States, the products of the Goldberger Works were from 1880 onwards exported to Western European countries, including Belgium, Italy and Great Britain.

At the turn of the century the rate of development in the Hungarian textile industry was greatly accelerated; nor did this expansion cease during the two world wars. In those four decades a number of large-scale factories—employing several thousand workers—were founded; works that have now become world renowned, the Kispest Textile Works, the Pápa Textile Factory, the Upjest Cotton Industry, the Hungaria Jacquard Factory, and the National Worsted and Weaving Factory, to mention but a few.

In 1938, the last year of peace, before the outbreak of the second world war, the Hungarian textile industry produced 146 millions sq.m. cotton, 15 million sq.m. woollen, 12 million sq.m. silk, and 10 million sq.m. of linen and hemp fabrics.

Following the second world war, in the course of which a considerable number of the textile works were destroyed or badly damaged, it was only with great difficulties that production could be launched again. In 1948, large-scale textile factories were nationalized and the Government carried out a gigantic investment programme, rebuilding, increasing and entirely modernizing the textile industry. New cotton mills were founded in the southern part of the country, in Szeged, at Kaposvár, and in one of the Budapest suburbs—at Pestszentlörinc. Also at Miskolc, one of the citadels of the Hungarian heavy industry, each factory specializing in its particular type of manufacture and being equipped with the most up-to-date machinery.

Ten years later, in 1958, as a result of this re-organization, the Hungarian textile industry had stepped up production to 300 million sq.m. of textile fabrics of all kinds. Of this quantity the cotton industry contributed the major portion, some 218 million sq.m. To put it into perspective, it amounts to an annual production of 22 sq.m. per head of the entire population, ensuring Hungary a high-ranking position amongst the textile manufacturing countries of the world today.

Nor does this increase in the quantity produced mean any decline in the traditional good quality of Hungarian textiles. Her fabrics hold their own in the competitive world markets by virtue of their durability as well as by their designs, so rich and novel in both pattern and colourings. The inexhaustible source of this abundance comes from her native peasant arts. The motifs of the gorgeous, colourful designs of world-famous hand-woven cloths, embroideries and peasant costumes of Kalocsa, Mezökóvesd and Sárköz are permanently drawn upon, adapted to modern taste and requirements and to the latest technical achievements in production methods.

The larger factories maintain designing studios of their own; the designers working in these studios incessantly study the ethnographical collections of Hungarian museums and visit the various regions of the country famous for their folk art. Mention should also be made of the company producing textile patterns entirely for the cotton industry, employing some 350 people. Though this company has its own designers producing patterns, its main job is the collection of designs prepared in the studios of the various textile factories, to preserve the formula of colourings and the engraved rollers, and also does considerable experimental manufacturing, supplying sample pieces and setting up sample ranges.

Not only the factories, but the Government itself, encourages the production of new and ever-improving designs. Each year there are competitions where the title 'The Most Beautiful Product of the Year' is annually awarded. Prizes totalling a hundred thousand forints are distributed among the designers of the finest patterns within the framework of this competition. Various adjudicating committees accept about three thousand designs annually, patterns that are to be manufactured in the following season.

In addition to design encouragement, great care is given to the development of modern methods of technology.

The characteristic feature of Hungarian textiles, apart from a very wide range, is quality —the variety of textiles manufactured is comprehensive, side by side with cotton, woollen, pure silk and linen goods are fabrics using synthetic fibres too, offering dress materials of all kinds, a rich variety of both printed and woven furnishing fabrics, garments for both under and outer wear, and knitwear too.

High-grade finishing methods, such as synthetic resin finishes, crease resistance and durable sheen are all used in the manufacturing processes. As a result of all these various developments a considerable proportion of the output of the Hungarian textile industry, i.e. about 100 million sq.m. of fabrics a year, are bought by foreign customers. The exportation of both knitted goods and wearing apparel is also advancing with giant strides.

This publication presents selections from the great variety of products the Hungarian textile industry can offer. To those interested, it gives a fair idea of its wide range of goods, and their design, but, alas, not of their lavishness of colour.

Descriptive Notes on the Illustrations

Figures 1, 3 *and* 4   Genuine Torontál carpets made by the Mezötur Co-operative have assimilated Oriental elements in addition to ancient Hungarian ornamental designs. The penetration of Oriental elements into Hungarian Folk Art is mainly due to the 150 years of Turkish conquest over the majority of Hungary's territory. It is for that matter a clue to the affinity between motifs used on carpets by Hungarians and other peoples (Roumanian, Bulgarian, Yugoslavian), since Turkish influence has been similarly strong in these countries.

Figure 2   Ancient motifs of Hungarian popular art (motifs of embroideries and hand-woven fabrics) are frequently adopted to lend novelty of patterns to Torontál carpets. This Torontál carpet with motifs taken from Hungarian folk art is made by the Békéscsaba Co-operative.

Figures 5 *and* 6 (*right*)   Peasant carpet, the design composed of traditional motifs used on felt cloaks worn by Hungarian shepherds. Hand-tufted, containing 100,000 tufts to the square metre. (*Left*) Peasant carpet, the design composed of motifs from the famous Buzsák embroideries. Hand-tufted, with 100,000 tufts to the square metre. Both designed by József Horváth.

Figures 7, 8 *and* 9   Hand-loomed Torontál-type woollen rugs with contemporary designs.

Figure 10   One of the most characteristic of Hungarian-bred animals is the racka sheep with its crewed horns. Up to the present its long, hard wool has been used only on the manufacture of cheap, rough blankets. Now the racka, considered a 'poor relative', has recently made some progress in the hierarchy of wool-bearing animals. This promotion has been due to the efforts of the chief engineer of the Kistarcsa Worsted Mill, a textile factory in the neighbourhood of Budapest. After a few years' experimenting he succeeded in producing a prototype of fine quality carpets made from racka-wool. This new product caught the fancy of a leading Hungarian industrial craftsman, and he devoted all his energies to the design of carpets, making full use of the possibilities inherent in this material. Today a special shop working in three shifts is devoted to the production of artistic racka carpets. Racka carpets are made in pure wool, by hand, in the same way as the finest Oriental carpets. The wool is undyed, colour effects being achieved by twenty different shades of natural fleece, ranging from white through every tone of grey to black. The striking varieties of colour lend themselves to the composition of patterns matching the modern lines of homes and furnishings. A tribute to the artistic qualities of racka carpets is the director's room in the Palace of Inventions in Berne is to be fitted with a racka carpet. This special carpet (*Figure* 10), of forty square metres, has been woven from seven shades of racka fleece, is made up of three million loops, and weighs 150 kilograms. To weave this carpet of unusual dimensions, a special loom had to be made. An outstanding craftsman, Karoly Plesznivy, designed the carpet, the design particularly enhanced by the specific qualities of the material. Symbols of peace, industry and trade around a stylized globe on which are displayed 19 of the best-known Hungarian trade marks.

Figures 11 *and* 12 Two more hand-loomed 'Racka' wool carpets, made in the Persian manner, but with contemporary designs.

Figure 13 Coarse linen curtain material, the design in ochre-red and black, by Marianne Szabó.

Figure 14 Here we show a hanging in a contemporary setting, a hand-woven material using synthetic fibres. Designed by Eva P. Szabó, textile designer, applied artist and leader of the Co-operative of Textile-Industrial Arts, Budapest, the design in black and gold, available on three different ground colours: eau-de-nil, red, or pastel blue. The divan-bed designed by Jozsef Peresztegi.

Figure 15 A group of upholstery fabrics, made for the Hotel Gellért, Budapest. All designed by Eva P. Szabó.

Figure 16 A pure silk dress fabric, designed by Marianne Szabó. This example in black on ochre.

Figure 17 Screen printed jute furnishing fabric, designed and produced by the Budakalász Textile Works.

Figure 18 Cambric dress material. Roller printed on pure cotton. The design in a golden yellow on a black ground. Designed and manufactured by Textile Dyeing Mill.

Figure 19 Cambric dress material. Roller printed on pure cotton. The design composed of an all-over series of geometric figures in the contemporary manner. Black on a light blue ground. Designed and manufactured by Hungarian Cotton Industry.

Figure 20   Roller printed pure cotton dress material in satin weave. Brilliantly coloured pebbles in grey and white, orange and chrome yellow, and orange and white make this a gay and colourful print. Designed and manufactured by Goldberger Textile Mills.

Figure 21   'Birch Tree' upholstery material made from silver-grey and gold synthetic fibres and black boucle yarn. Designed by Eva P. Szabó.

Figure 22   Six-colour screen printed pure cotton fabric on white ground. This example in bright colours: rose red, chrome yellow, emerald green, bright blue, crimson and black. Designed and manufactured by the Goldberger Textile Works.

Figure 23   Roller printed pure cotton dress material in satin weave. Designed and produced by the Goldberger Textile Works.

Figure 24   Pure cotton furnishing fabric of linen type; roller printed. This example in grey, green, saxe blue and navy on a white ground. Designed and produced by the Goldberger Textile Works.

Figure 25   Roller printed pure cotton dress fabric in satin weave. Designed and manufactured at the Goldberger Textile Works.

Figure 26   Printed linen. Design in black on an ochreous coloured ground, by Marianne Szabó.

Figure 27   'Roza'. Pure cotton fabric with embossed effect finish. Manufactured and designed by Goldberger Textile Works.

Figure 28   From the Kispeth Textile Factory comes this screen printed furnishing fabric with a very pleasing period floral design on an all-cotton crêpe. 48 and 51 inch widths.

Figure 29   Produced by the Györ Flax Weavers for ladies' skirts, this colour woven cloth is composed on cotton and flax. Available in 31 and 35 inch widths.

Figure 30   Showing a Matyó needlewoman from Mezökövesd wearing the traditional costume in front of embroidered pillows piled upon her bed. The Matyó art has been lately adapted as hand-embroidered ornament on so-called Hungarian 'peasant blouses' made of Swiss voile, rayon georgette or crêpe-de-chine.

Figure 31   (*Right*) Sárköv cover with 'pick-up' embroidery. Variety of pattern is the characteristic feature of Sárköv hand-woven textiles. There are so many ways to reproduce the typical Sárköv pattern that hardly ever are two identical pieces encountered.

The ancient black and white colour scheme has been replaced by red with some white and black, combinations of green, brown and yellow are also in favour. (*Left*) Hand-woven Palóc cover. The land of the Palócs is famous for its popular arts and crafts. Hand-loom cotton fabrics produced in a variety of colourings are widely used as table covers, curtains and other items of interior decoration.

Figure 32 Cover with felt appliqué. Felt appliqué is a technique used in the past as ornament on shepherds' cloaks. Today this art has been revived on fancy articles for decorative purposes.

Figure 33 Matyó table-runner. Matyó women embellish covers and cushions with brightly covered embroidery. Patterns are spread all over the background. Most characteristic is the effect produced by flowers of every shade of red, ranging from pink to claret, harmoniously interwoven with deep green foliage.

Figure 34 Kalocsa cover. The brightly embroidered national costumes of Kalocsa evoke the flower gardens of the Hungarian Lowlands. A contemporary field of utilization for these patterns has been found in home decoration, dressing table sets, covers, etc.

Figure 35 Tura table mats. The Palóc population of Tura, a small village on the river Galgóc, still wear their national costume. An embroidered shawl, gathered in plaits about the shoulders, is a characteristic piece of their Sunday attire. The white shawl is embroidered in white, with two red motifs surmounting the parts crossed over the breast. Handkerchief patterns, rhythmically repeated motifs or the Tura national dress, are particularly decorative on modern table cloths and mats.

Figures 36 *and* 37 (*Top*) Halas lace cover. The Halas lace is a needlepoint variety, the most beautiful of all Hungarian laces. A stout thread or cordonnet is employed to outline the pattern, the ornamental filling of which comprises a single thread with innumerable stitches. (*Bottom*) Triangular kerchief from Hövej. Popular embroideries of Hövej are among the prettiest needleworks made in the Rábaköz region. Essentially they are a combination of flat embroidery and openings, the large openings being filled with a special needlepoint called spider. There exist some 35 varieties of spiders. Practically all the womenfolk in the village of Hövej make or design embroidery. The triangular shawl is a classical example of ancient style and popular decorative elements. The border and the corner bows of the embroidery are characteristic.

Figures 38 *and* 39 (*Top*) Bobbin-lace mat. Making bobbin lacework is a common occupation in Hungarian villages. Ancient folk motifs lend the patterns a truly Hungarian flavour. (*Bottom*) Drawn-thread table mat. White embroidery combined with delicate drawn-thread technique applied to decorate small mats, d'oylies and napkins, framed in crocheted lace.

Figures 40 and 41 (*Top*) Halas lace mat. See the explanatory description of Halas lace with figure 36. (*Bottom*) Bobbin lace mat. See also figure 38.

Figures 42 and 43 (*Top*) Afternoon tea-cloth with matching napkins. The diaphanous needlework of this set is a version of the Hövej 'cat's paw' pattern. See also figure 37. (*Bottom*) Three-piece dressing table set from Hövej.

Figure 44 Afternoon tea-cloth and matching napkins with tulle appliqué. Tulle appliqué is an old but popular technique. Originally the fabric was folded and recurring patterns cut out with a single clipping. The elements are attached to the fine tulle foundation with delicate hem-stitches so as to give a delicate lace effect.

Figures 45 and 46 (*Top*) Screen printed cotton satin. Designed and produced by the Goldberger Textile Factory. (*Bottom*) Multi-coloured dress fabrics for summer wear. Designed by Hungarian Cotton Industry Studio.

Figures 47 and 48 (*Top*) This novelty design is one of many fashion fabrics from the Goldberger Textile Factory Studio. This particular pattern is mainly intended for the younger person. (*Bottom*) While from the Kispest Textile Factory Studio comes this contemporary design 51-inch fabric, suitable for loose covers and general furnishing schemes.

Figures 49 and 50 (*Left*) An example of the many lingerie materials produced at the Textile Dyeing Factory. (*Right*) Screen print on cotton from Goldberger Textile Factory. Designed in their own studio.

Figures 51 and 52 (*Top*) This fabric designed mainly for children's wear, also eminently suitable for summer and beach wear. From the Goldberger Textile Factory. (*Bottom*) A gay design printed on flannel for babywear. Designed and produced by the Hungarian Cotton Industry.

Figure 53 Jacquard table-cloth, available in cotton, all-linen, or part linen. 51 by 51 inches. Produced by Budakalász Textile Works.

Figures 54 and 55 (*Left*) All-cotton colour woven table-cloth; colour fast. Made in 35 by 35 inches or 45 by 45 inches. Produced by Cotton Weavers. (*Right*) Screen printed linen table-cloth, size 51 by 51 inches. Manufactured by Budakalász Textile Works.

Figures 56 and 57 (*Top*) Three woven materials in varying colours and patterns from Pápa Textile Factory. (*Bottom*) All-linen screen printed table cloth, 51 inches square. Produced by Budakalász Textile Works.

Figures 58 and 59 (*Top*) Part linen roller-printed tea-cloth material, 19 inches wide. Produced by Textile Dyeing Factory. (*Bottom*) Modern bed damasks produced by National Cotton Weavers.

Figure 60 Roller printed oil-cloth with plain or napped back, spread with linseed or p.v.c. Produced by Cotton Weavers' and Artificial Leather Factory, Györ.

Figures 61 and 62 (*Left*) 'Dream', an all-cotton jacquard towel. (*Right*) All-cotton colour woven Terry towelling for bathing wraps, etc. Width 59 inches. Both produced by Cotton Weavers.

Figures 63 and 64 (*Top*) This winter-wear flannel is napped on both sides, intended for morning dresses, indoor frocks and pyjamas. Designed and produced by Kispest Textile Factory. (*Bottom*) Colour woven pyjama fabric from Pápa Textile Factory.

Figure 65 Floral all-over design made of all-silk thread; width 35 inches. Screen printed, designed and produced at the Goldberger Textile Factory.

Figures 66, 67, 68 and 69 (*Top left*) Frock and cape made of violet beige patterned boucle cloth. (*Top right*) Calico frock with a Biedermeyer (early nineteenth century) design on a white ground, seamed or edged in the colour of the pattern. (*Bottom left*) Hand-embroidered evening gown. (*Bottom right*) Here is an elegant three-piece suit.

Figures 70, 71, 72 and 73 (*Top left*) For ski-ing comes this new-styled *ensemble*. (*Top right*) Black and white pied-de-poule riding jacket with hazel-coloured Jodhpurs for the horsewoman. (*Bottom left*) All-linen for the beach; grey-white striped coat with blouse and slacks in different shades of brick red. (*Bottom right*) This casual or play-suit comprising a napped or brushed wool jumper with grey and violet stripes, over a grey jersey sleeveless pullover, and grey jersey slacks.

Figures 74, 75, 76 and 77 (*Top left*) Fully fashioned all-wool cardigan. (*Top right*) Ladies' jumper in a simple but smart pattern. (*Bottom left*) An all-wool cardigan with raglan sleeves, made on a flat-bed knitter. (*Bottom right*) Fully fashioned all-wool twin-set for the teen-ager.

Figures 78 and 79 A selection of woollen and mixed suitings in various weights and 54 to 58 inch widths from different mills in Hungary.

ILLUSTRATIONS

FIG. I. FROM THE MEZÖTUR CO-OPERATIVE

FIG. 2. FROM THE BÉKÉSCSABA CO-OPERATIVE

FIG. 3. FROM THE MEZŐTUR CO-OPERATIVE

FIG. 4. FROM THE MEZÖTUR CO-OPERATIVE

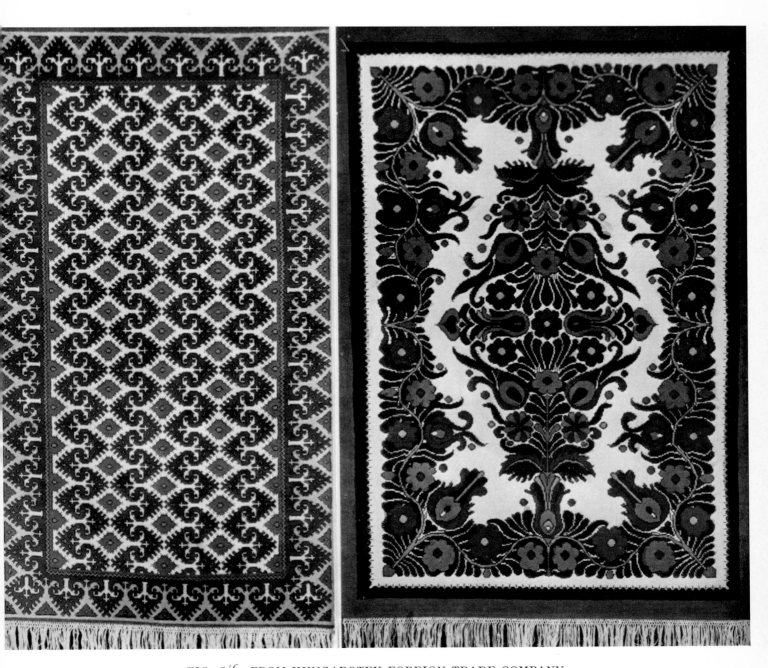

FIG. 5/6. FROM HUNGAROTEX FOREIGN TRADE COMPANY

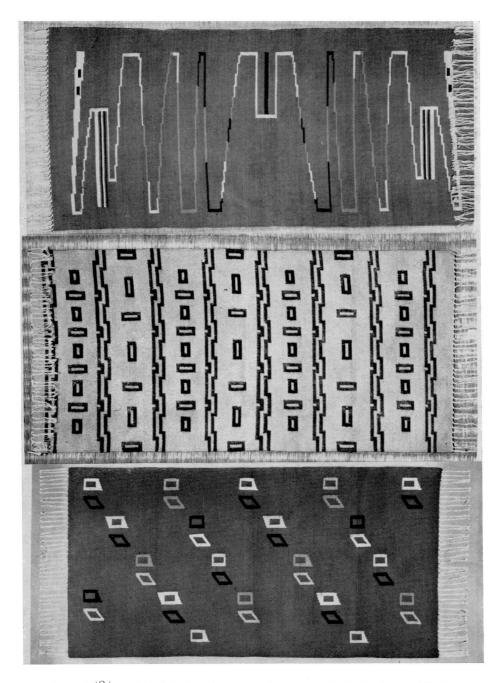

FIG. 7/8/9. FROM HUNGAROTEX FOREIGN TRADE COMPANY

FIG. 10. FROM HUNGAROTEX FOREIGN TRADE COMPANY

FIG. II. FROM HUNGAROTEX FOREIGN TRADE COMPANY

FIG. 12. FROM HUNGAROTEX FOREIGN TRADE COMPANY

FIG. 13. DESIGNED BY MARIANNE SZABÓ

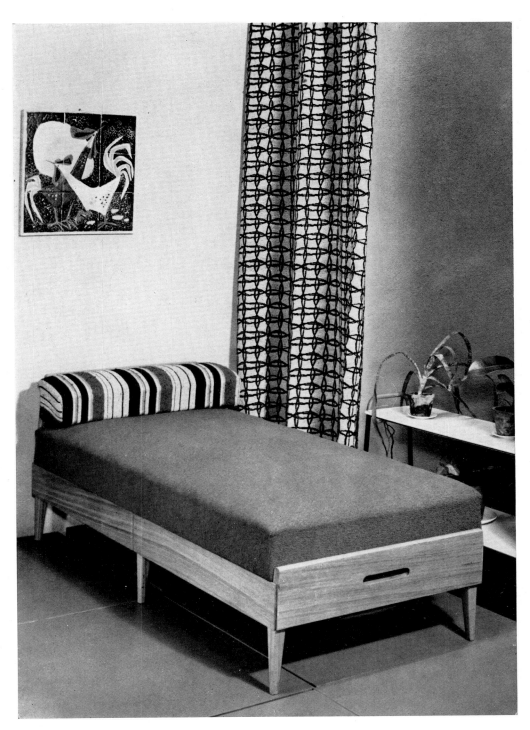

FIG. 14. DESIGNED BY EVA P. SZABÓ

FIG. 15. TEXTILES DESIGNED BY EVA P. SZABÓ FOR HOTEL GELLÉRT

FIG. 16. DESIGNED BY MARIANNE SZABÓ

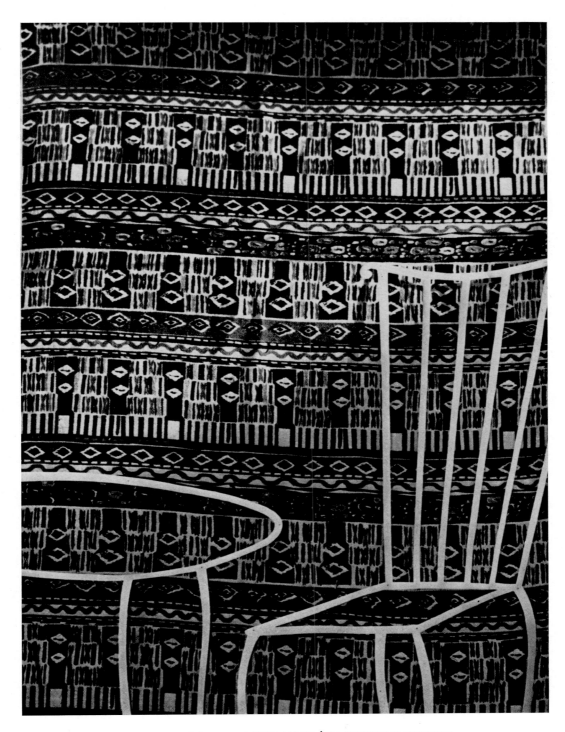

FIG. 17. FROM THE BUDAKALÁSZ TEXTILE WORKS

FIG. 18. FROM TEXTILE DYEING MILL

FIG. 19. FROM HUNGARIAN COTTON INDUSTRY

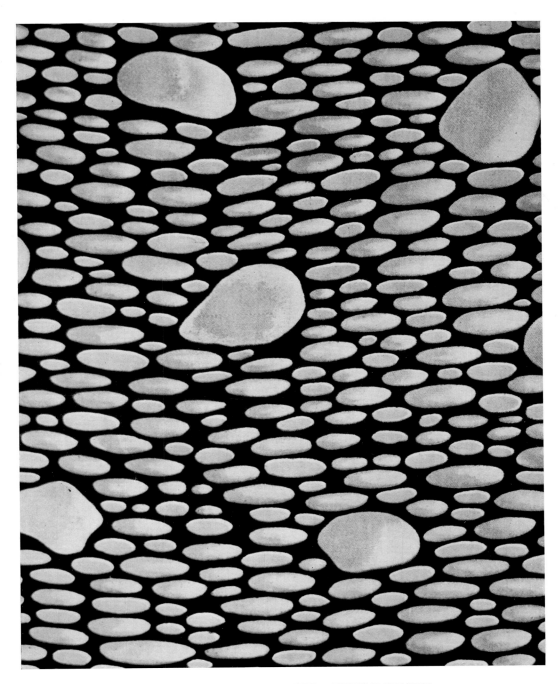

FIG. 20. FROM GOLDBERGER TEXTILE WORKS

FIG. 21. DESIGNED BY EVA P. SZABÓ

FIG. 22. FROM GOLDBERGER TEXTILE WORKS

FIG. 23. FROM GOLDBERGER TEXTILE WORKS

FIG. 24. FROM GOLDBERGER TEXTILE WORKS

FIG. 25. FROM GOLDBERGER TEXTILE WORKS

FIG. 26. DESIGNED BY MARIANNE SZABÓ

FIG. 27. FROM GOLDBERGER TEXTILE WORKS

FIG. 28. FROM KISPETH TEXTILE FACTORY

FIG. 29. FROM GYÖR FLAX WEAVERS

FIG. 30. TRADITIONAL DRESS FROM MEZŐKÖVESD

FIG. 31. SARKÖZ & PALÓC HANDWOVEN COVERS

FIG. 32. COVER WITH FELT APPLIQUÉ

FIG. 33. MATYÓ TABLE RUNNER

FIG. 34. KALOCSA EMBROIDERED COVER

FIG. 35. TURA TABLE MATS

FIG. 36/37. *(top)* HALAS LACE COVER *(bottom)* HÖVEJ KERCHIEF

FIG. 38/39. *(top)* BOBBIN LACE MAT *(bottom)* DRAWN THREAD MAT

FIG. 40/41. *(top)* HALAS LACE MAT *(bottom)* BOBBIN LACE MAT

FIG. 42/43. HÖVEJ NEEDLEWORK

FIG. 44. TABLE CLOTH WITH TULLE APPLIQUÉ

FIG. 45/46. *(top)* FROM GOLDBERGER TEXTILE FACTORY
(bottom) FROM HUNGARIAN COTTON INDUSTRY STUDIO

FIG. 47/48. *(top)* FROM GOLDBERGER TEXTILE FACTORY
(bottom) FROM KISPEST TEXTILE FACTORY

FIG. 49/50. *(left)* FROM TEXTILE DYEING FACTORY *(bottom)* FROM GOLDBERGER TEXTILE FACTORY

FIG. 51/52. *(top)* FROM GOLDBERGER TEXTILE FACTORY
(bottom) FROM HUNGARIAN COTTON INDUSTRY

FIG. 53. FROM BUDAKALÁSZ TEXTILE WORKS

FIG. 54/55. *(left)* FROM COTTON WEAVERS *(right)* FROM BUDAKALÁSZ TEXTILE WORKS

FIG. 56/57. *(top)* FROM PÁPA TEXTILE FACTORY
(bottom) FROM BUDAKALÁSZ TEXTILE WORKS

FIG. 58/59. *(top)* FROM TEXTILE DYEING FACTORY
(bottom) FROM NATIONAL COTTON WEAVERS

FIG. 60. FROM COTTON WEAVERS' & ARTIFICIAL LEATHER FACTORY, GYÖR

FIG. 61/62. FROM COTTON WEAVERS

FIG. 63/64. *(top)* FROM KISPEST TEXTILE FACTORY
(bottom) FROM PÁPA TEXTILE FACTORY

FIG. 65. FROM GOLDBERGER TEXTILE FACTORY

FIG. 66/67/68/69. EXAMPLES OF HUNGARIAN FASHION GOODS

FIG. 70/71/72/73. EXAMPLES OF HUNGARIAN FASHION GOODS

FIG. 74/75/76/77. EXAMPLES OF HUNGARIAN KNITWEAR

FIG. 78/79. SELECTION OF WOOLLEN AND MIXED SUITINGS